Contents

4

Foreword

Professor Caroline Fennell
Law Faculty, UCC

IT IS A GREAT PLEASURE to be invited to write the introduction to this timely and important document: not just because of what it offers as a practical and up to date guide which is value enough in itself, but also because it represents the fruit of a wonderful synergy between town and gown in the form of the long standing, and I would hope mutually beneficial relationship, between the Sexual Violence Centre and UCC Law Faculty. For many years we have been committed to facilitating the engagement of students, staff and researchers with those working in the area of victim support, and the Sexual Violence Centre has been to the forefront in facilitating visits, briefing students and engaging in joint research. The creation of a specific Centre for Criminal Justice and Human Rights in the Faculty in 2006 will no doubt help to further strengthen this relationship in the future. This Guide is another visible manifestation of the students and staff of UCC Law Faculty together with the staff of the Sexual Violence Centre, at their initiative and invitation, co-operating in a manner which will very directly affect and empower those caught within the criminal justice system. Bridging the gap between the practice and theory of law has long been part of the distinctive mission of the Law Faculty, and this guide is a testament to what can be achieved if those of us working in criminal justice work together in partnership. It is a shining example of the academy working together with the community; and it bodes well for the ongoing meaningful and successful engagement of the University community in Cork with the 'real world' outside the gates.

Professor Caroline Fennell
Law Faculty, UCC

5

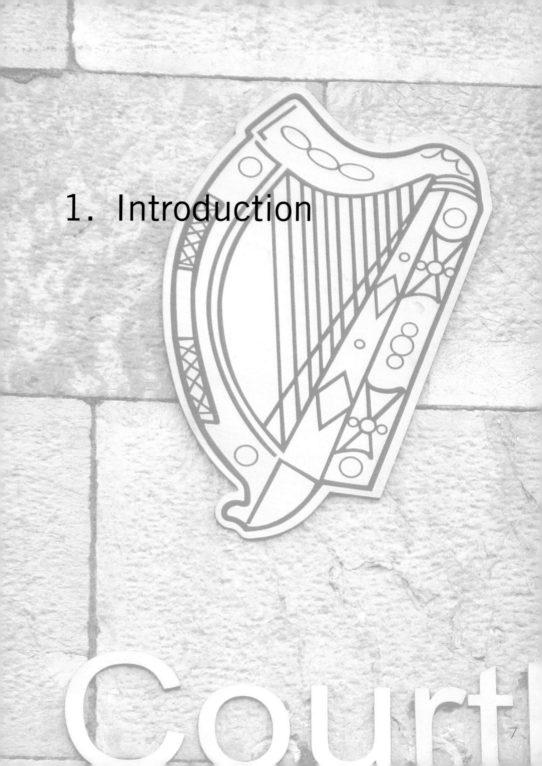

1. Introduction

Chapter 1

Introduction

Mary Crilly
Director, Sexual Violence Centre Cork

I HAVE BEEN INVOLVED with the Sexual Violence Centre (Cork Rape Crisis Centre) since 1983. In that time, I have accompanied many women to Court and spoken with others about their experiences within the legal system. Considering there have been many changes in Irish law over the past twenty years, such as the Criminal Law Rape Amendment Act 1981 and 1990, the Criminal Law Sexual Offences Act 1993 and 2006, it would be reasonable to expect that more victims would feel that justice was done and that more offenders would be called to account. This however has not been the case. The conviction rate for sexual violence in Ireland is 5%. Of sex offences reported to the Gardaí, 16% end up in court. The experience of the Sexual Violence Centre Cork and Rape Crisis Centres nationwide is that less than 25% of victims who avail of our services report to the Gardaí. There are countless victims who do not avail of our services, so the true incidence of sexual violence in Ireland is greater than official statistics indicate. The Central Statistics Office figures state that there were 1,580 sexual offences reported in Ireland in 2006. Research in Ireland (The SAVI Report) indicate that 1 in 5 women experience Sexual Violence as adults. The issue of Sexual Violence is an issue that concerns everyone, all of us will have been a victim or know someone who has – even if we don't know! On the surface therefore, this guide is relevant only to the minority of victims who have contact with the Criminal Justice System. My hope is, and it is a hope that has kept me working in the field for 24 years, is that more victims will receive the services they need and deserve both from professional support services and the Criminal Justice System.

For many years, I had hoped that someone would produce a guide for victims, their families and friends, for professionals and others who encounter victims – a guide that would be informative for all who read it. While every victim of sexual violence is an individual with a different and traumatic experience, the questions that victims have asked and the answers they need, share common ground. This guide represents my attempt to be "that someone" to produce that guide. My hope is that this guide will serve to outline the Criminal Justice System in Ireland as it relates to the crime of sexual violence – that it may demystify what is by its nature a complex system – that it will answer questions for victims and others and thereby help inform their decisions to report to the Gardaí or to seek professional help and support. I have made every effort to ensure the accuracy of the contents in the guide and am aware that it may contain a level of error, that more clarity in some areas may be required and that there may be omissions. My request, to you the reader, is to forward comments and suggestions to me, for inclusion in later editions of the guide. If you have any questions that are not addressed in the guide or if you require more detailed information, please feel free to contact me by phone or e-mail.

Even as this publication goes to print, there are legislative developments in the pipeline on the issue of sex trafficking – Ireland's newest form of sexual violence and exploitation; and the Sexual Violence Centre has this year begun to offer services and supports to victims of sex trafficking.

Who this Guide is for

This guide has been written primarily for victims of sexual violence, and the friends and family members who support them. The issue of Child Sexual Abuse was outside the scope of this edition, which concentrates on Adult Victims of Child Sexual Abuse and teenage and adult victims of rape and sexual assault. In the guide, the victim is referred to as "she" and the offender as "he", as this is the most common case reported to the Gardaí. Many victims of sexual assault are male. The Sexual Violence Centre Cork and several Rape Crisis Centres provide services to male and female victims.

This guide is also aimed at personnel working the Criminal Justice System and Support Services to enhance their understanding of the role of each agency. It is also written with professionals, voluntary organisations and community agencies in mind, that they will have a guide to refer to should victims disclose to them.

If you are a Victim:

I am writing this piece for the victims of Sexual Assault, who read this Guide, in the hope that I can encourage you to seek help and support. You may feel there is no point in talking and feel that speaking about the assault won't change what has happened. You may feel that you are coping well or you may feel you are not coping and seeking professional support in the form of counselling may feel daunting. You may feel guilty and ashamed about what happened and fear that you won't be believed or that you will be judged. If the abuse happened a long time ago, you may also feel that you should be "over it". You may feel that what happened to you is not as bad as what has happened to others.

I know it is difficult to make the decision to seek help but please do – at the very least, tell someone, a trusted friend or family member. Living with the effects of sexual assault is not easy. You may feel trapped in a cycle of guilt, guilty because you were abused and guilty because you cant "get over it". Nobody asks to be raped or abused and the responsibility lies solely with the offender. Counselling can make a difference. Why carry this anymore? Why let the abuser take more of your life? You are important, special and innocent and maybe now is the time to say "enough is enough".

If you are the Family or Friend of a Victim:

Most families and friends I have met over the years feel helpless and powerless and are unsure how to help and support a loved one who has been raped or abused. It is important to remember that there is no typical response to sexual assault. Frequently victims experience disbelief and attempt to "get back to normal", as a coping mechanism. She may not want to make a report about the assault, and may not want to talk about it.

You may feel an urgency to make a report and worry that this is going to have an effect on the rest of her life. You may know the assailant and want to confront him but you have been asked to say nothing. You don't know whether to ask the person about the assault or not. Its hard isn't it? It is vital however that you believe the victim and that she knows you are there for her whenever she is ready and that you support any decision she makes. It is also important that you get support for yourself. The Support Services can provide support to you too.

Immediate effects of A Sexual Assault include:
- shock and withdrawal – may appear frozen
- panic and confusion
- dwelling on details of the rape or sexual assault
- recurrent flash backs
- sleeplessness and nightmares
- startles easily
- inappropriately calm and rational
- obsessive washing
- physical trauma

Longterm effects include:
- mood swings
- intrusive recollections
- self blame / guilt
- fear and anxiety
- difficulty in trusting
- poor memory and concentration
- sexual difficulties
- depression
- substance abuse
- self loathing
- suicide ideation

With support from family and friends and professional support, the majority of victims eventually "pick up the pieces of their lives".

If a Victim discloses to you:

- Believe the person
- Listen to what they are telling you
- Affirm the person
- Be aware how difficult it is to disclose
- Reassure the person they are doing the right thing in disclosing
- Respect the persons right to privacy and confidentiality
- Encourage the person to disclose as much as they can but do not press for details
- Try to find out who else knows to establish if they have support
- Encourage them to consider reporting to the Gardaí
- Encourage them to seek professional support

Acknowledgments

This guide would not have been possible without the support and expertise of many people, too many to mention here, from those who were "cornered" by my questions and repeated requests for clarifications, to those who were commandeered to read and comment on draft after draft. There are two people in particular, who made the guide possible: firstly, Detective Inspector Mick Kelleher who was a friend to me and an ally to many victims of Sexual Violence in Cork and who is now retired from the force, secondly, Dr. Shane Kilcommins for his support, encouragement and his legal expertise. I also wish to mention Shane's students Susan Leahy and Susan O Sullivan.

I wish to thank the staff of the Sexual Violence Centre and my family and friends who have waited a long time for this project to be completed.

Above all, I wish to express my gratitude to the victims of sexual violence that it has been my privilege to meet over many years – both those who reported and those who did not. Their courage is my constant source of inspiration.

Publication of the Guide was made possible by funding from the Department of Justice Equality and Law Reform, the Department of Social, Community and Family Affairs, and Cork City Partnership.

Disclaimer

The information available in this booklet is intended as a guide only. It does not purport to be, nor should it be relied upon, as advice. Those seeking legal advice on a matter affecting them should consult their own legal advisor.

Mary Crilly
Director, Sexual Violence Centre Cork
mcrilly@sexualviolence.ie
1800 496 496
December 2007

2. Reporting Sexual Violence: The Agencies Involved

Chapter 2

Reporting Sexual Violence: The Agencies Involved

There are a number of agencies involved in cases of reported sexual violence. This chapter outlines the role of these agencies.

An Garda Siochana

One of the main roles of An Garda Siochana, Ireland's national police service, is to detect crime and to bring perpetrators to justice. An Garda Siochana is the sole investigative agency of sexual crimes. They are the first point of contact to report rape, sexual assault and past sexual abuse. The Gardaí investigate reports of sexual crimes by gathering forensic evidence and documentary evidence. Forensic evidence consists of physical evidence such as fingerprints, blood, hairs, cuts, bruises. Documentary evidence consists of witness statements, photographs, e-mails, text messages and any video evidence from CCTV. The Gardaí are obliged to investigate reported crime as quickly as possible and to compile and forward an investigation file on the case to the Office of the Director of Public Prosecutions. A number of Gardaí will be involved in the investigation of every case - detectives, scene of crime officers and an investigating Garda. The investigating Garda is responsible for keeping the victim informed as to how the case is proceeding. The victim will be given the name and telephone contact number of the investigating Garda.

Office of the Director of Public Prosecutions (DPP)

The Office of the DPP is an independent body in charge of prosecuting criminal offences in Ireland. The Office of the DPP decides whether to charge a person with a criminal offence, what the charges will be and in which court the case will be heard. The Office of the DPP decides, on behalf of the State, to prosecute a crime. A victim of crime cannot take criminal proceedings against a perpetrator. A victim of crime can only take a civil case against a perpetrator. If the Office of the DPP decides that a person is to be charged, the Office decides on the offence / offences that the accused will be charged with. Offences can range from indecent assault to aggravated sexual assault to rape. The severity of the charge / charges, dictate the Court in which the case will be heard. Within the office of the DPP is the Solicitors Division headed by the Chief Prosecution Solicitor. The staff of this division prepares the case for court by compiling what is termed the Book of Evidence and represents the DPP in all courts in Dublin. Local State Solicitors represent the DPP in courts outside Dublin.

Sexual Assault Treatment Units (SATUs)

SATUs are specialised units, based in hospitals where Forensic Medical Examinations (FME) are carried out. These examinations are performed by trained medical personnel. The purpose of an FME is to gather forensic evidence. It is important that a Forensic Medical Examination is performed as soon as possible after a sexual attack. If too much time has elapsed, the forensic evidence will have deteriorated. After a lapse of 7 days after the assault, little if any forensic evidence can be gathered. Forensic evidence is stored and sealed in a Sexual Offences Examination Kit. The Kit is handed to the Gardaí who are present in the Unit during the FME and forwarded by the Gardaí to the Forensic Science Laboratory, which is based in Dublin. The experience of a Forensic Medical Examination can be very unpleasant for a victim as it involves the taking of internal as well as external swab samples. The victim is also examined for lacerations, bruises, bites and other injuries. The clothing that the victim wore at the time of the sexual assault is also sent for analysis. Clothing may contain valuable evidence or may have been ripped or damaged. When the victims clothing is retained for evidence, the victim is provided with a track suit and trainers at the SATU. Medical personnel provide emergency contraception and test for Sexually Transmitted Infections. The victim is given an appointment to return to the Unit for the results of these tests. The victim will not receive the results of the forensic examination, as this evidence might form part of a future court case. Victims who require any other medical attention are referred to Accident & Emergency Departments or to their General Practitioner.

Support Services

Rape Crisis Centres provide services to victims of sexual violence – both to victims who report to the Gardaí and those who don't. Approximately 75% of victims who avail of services have not made a report to the Gardaí. Rape Crisis Centres provide a range of services to victims including: information, support, advocacy, liaison, accompaniment, counselling, and preparation of Victim Impact Reports. Rape Crisis Centres also provide services to families and friends of victims, to professionals and others who encounter victims of sexual violence in the course of their work or otherwise. Centres provide information to victims on the reporting process, the criminal justice system and all issues relating to court cases. Centres are on-call to meet with victims when they undergo a Forensic Medical Examination and provide a court accompaniment service. The Rape Crisis Centre in Cork changed its name to the Sexual Violence Centre Cork in 2004, to more accurately reflect the range of services provided.

The Courts

Courts involved in the prosecution of Sexual Violence in Ireland:

1. The District Court

Cases heard in the District Court are categorised as "less serious crimes". Cases are heard in front of a judge. There is no jury in a District Court. The maximum sentence that a judge can hand down in this court is 12 months for any single offence. Serious sexual assault cases are not heard in the District Court, but this is the court the person to be charged with the offence, first attends. Both the District Court Judge and the accused are presented with the Book of Evidence. The judge will examine the Book of Evidence and decide if the case is ready to proceed.

2. The Circuit Court

Cases which begin in the District Court can be sent forward to the Circuit Court for trial. Trials in this court are heard in front of a judge and jury.

3. The Central Criminal Court

The High Court tries criminal cases outside the jurisdiction of the Circuit Court. The Central Criminal Court is a specialised court of the High Court that hears cases of rape, aggravated sexual assault and murder. This court consists of a judge or judges of the High Court and cases are heard in front of a jury.

4. The Court of Criminal Appeal

The Court of Criminal Appeal hears appeals against the convictions and sentences of convicted sex offenders and appeals against sentences that are viewed as too lenient by the DPP.

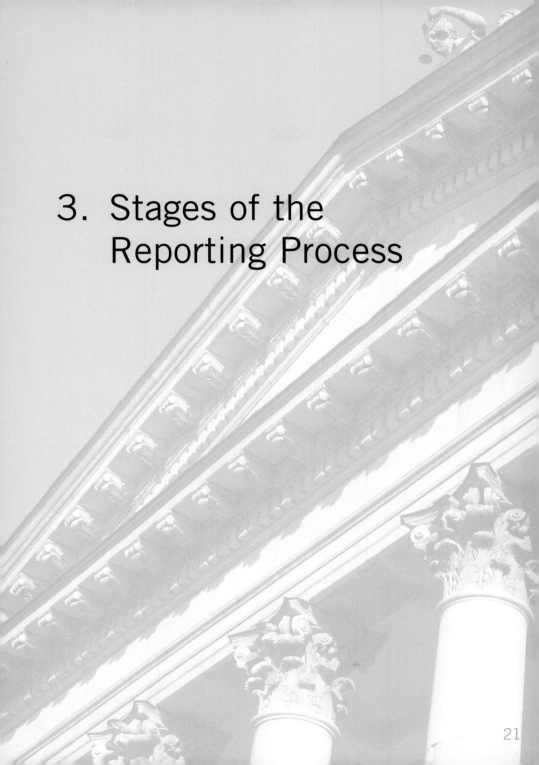

3. Stages of the Reporting Process

1 Reporting to the Gardaí

2 Identification of Assailant

3 File goes to DPP

6 The Trial

5 The Plea

4 Pre-Trial

7 Verdict

8 Sentencing

9 Sex Offender Register

10 Appeal

Chapter 3
Stages of the Reporting Process

1. Reporting to the Gardaí

The decision to report an incident of sexual assault or rape can be difficult for a victim. Frequently, they will be in a state of shock and trying to come to terms with what has happened to them. 80% of victims of rape and sexual assault know their assailant and may blame themselves in part, for what happened. The victim may fear that they won't be believed, and that everyone will know what has happened to them. It is important however to report the assault to the Gardaí at the earliest opportunity so that physical and documentary evidence can be collected.

The Gardaí can be contacted day or night by phoning the emergency number 999 or 112. Alternatively, contact can be made by phone or in person to the local Garda Station. Opening times of local Garda Stations vary from location to location. A victim may prefer to be interviewed by a female Garda and the Gardaí will facilitate this request. The Gardaí will interview the victim at the Garda Station or at an agreed location, such as the victim's home, if requested. Anglesea Street Garda Station, the Cork Divisional Headquarters, has a designated room used only for interviewing victims of sexual crimes. The Garda Station nearest to where the assault occurred has responsibility to investigate the case. If a victim is living in Cork and the assault happened in Dublin, then the Dublin Gardaí investigate the case, and vice versa.

Initially the investigating Garda will ask for details of the assault and a description of the attacker (if the person is unknown to the victim). The victim will be asked to identify the location of the assault. If the Gardaí believe that evidence can be collected at the location of the assault, the location can be designated a crime scene, permitting the Gardaí to cordon off and examine the location for a period of 24 hours.

If the victim was assaulted within the previous seven days, the Gardaí will arrange a Forensic Medical Examination at the nearest SATU, immediately. If it is not possible to arrange an immediate FME, the Gardaí will gather some forensic evidence from the victim, using the Early Evidence Kits, which are available in all Garda Stations. The Gardaí will drive the victim to the SATU and remain in the Unit until the FME is complete.

The Gardaí will want to take a statement from the victim as early as possible, after the assault. This statement will be very detailed. It is called a **formal statement of complaint**. This statement can take several hours to complete. The victim will be asked to repeat the details of the assault to ensure that there are no inaccuracies or omissions in the statement. The victim will be asked questions in relation to her movements before and after the sexual assault. If the attacker is known to the victim, the victim will be questioned about her relationship with him. At the end of the interview, the victim will be asked to sign the document, written by the Garda, that contains all the details of the assault. It is critical that the victim read this document carefully and make any necessary changes before signing it. When the victim signs the document, it becomes her **statement**. If the victim remembers other details about the assault at a later stage she can make a supplementary statement. The statement will be central in the event of the case going to court. The victim is entitled to a copy of the statement. If the case is to go to court the defence will receive a copy of the statement. The victim will be closely questioned and challenged in court, on the basis of the statement.

Information on all reported crime in Ireland is now entered into the Garda PULSE system (Police Using Leading Systems Effectively). Within a short time of reporting a crime the victim should receive a letter from the Gardaí.

This letter will contain the contact name and phone number of the Investigating Garda, the Pulse Incident Number and a list of support services. A victim can contact any Gardaí station with this Incident Number to inquire on the progress of a case. A victim will receive a second letter to inform her of the arrest or charging of their attacker, if any, when this has occurred.

2. Identification of Assailant

Questioning the assailant

There is often an assumption that when a victim has identified or named the attacker and has completed the statement to the Gardaí that the attacker will be arrested by the Gardaí and questioned, immediately. This is rarely the case unless the Gardaí are of the opinion that the attacker may flee the jurisdiction. In most cases of sexual violence, weeks or months will pass before the Gardaí approach the attacker. The Gardaí work to build the case, before questioning the attacker and therefore wait for forensic examination results to come back from the laboratory, and for witness statements to be completed. Another reason for delay is the involvement of investigating Gardaí in other cases. Every case of reported sexual violence is different and this accounts for variations in the time it takes to investigate cases.

A suspect detained in Garda custody for questioning has the right of reasonable access to a solicitor. If the suspect is under 18 years a parent or guardian is contacted immediately. The suspect usually can be held in custody for an initial 12 hours and this can be extended to 24 hours. The interviews are all video taped although the statements are still handwritten. The Gardaí need written permission to take intimate forensic samples e.g., blood, pubic hair etc. The suspect can refuse to give his consent to the taking of an intimate sample. A refusal to co-operate, however, can be noted in any subsequent court proceedings. During the 12 or 24 hours of detention the Gardaí may be in contact with the Office of Director of Public Prosecution to inform them how the investigation is proceeding. The suspect may be charged in court immediately or may be released without charge. If he is brought to court and charged the judge may release him on bail while the Book of Evidence is being prepared.

3. File goes to DPP

In all serious crimes," indictable offences" as they are termed, the Gardaí on completing their investigation, send the completed file to the Office of the Director of Public Prosecutions. The Office of the DPP decides whether to charge a person with a criminal offence, what the charges will be and in which court the case will be tried. The DPP's decision can take several months. Files concerning sexual offences generally take longer to consider partly because of their relative complexity and partly because further information/clarification is frequently sought from Gardaí prior to a decision being made. If the DPP decides that there is not enough evidence to prosecute then the Gardaí will inform the victim of this decision. The DPP does not meet with victims of crime and it is the policy of the DPP not to inform victims of the reasons why a case is not being taken. This policy is presently under review (2007). When the DPP makes a decision not to proceed with a case, this can be traumatic for the victim. For the victim, it will feel like she has not been believed and her attacker will not be answerable for the crime. Even when the DPPs Office believes the victims story, the evidence may simply not be strong enough to convince a jury, beyond reasonable doubt. In many situations, there is very little physical or forensic evidence and the case would rest on the victims word against the accused. The burden of proof in criminal cases is "beyond reasonable doubt".

If the DPP's decision is to prosecute a case, the victim is informed of this decision by the Gardaí. The Solicitors Division of the Office of the DPP, headed by the Chief Prosecution Solicitor Office prepare the case for prosecution by compiling the **Book of Evidence** for court. The statutory period granted for the preparation of a Book of Evidence is 42 days (which can be extended) from the date the accused is charged. The amount of time required to prepare the Book of Evidence can vary greatly depending on the complexity of the case.

4. Pre-Trial

Charge and Arrest

When the Gardaí are informed of the decision of the DPP to prosecute a case and of the charge / charges that have been levied against the suspect, the Gardaí arrange to arrest the suspect and bring him before the District Court. In the District Court the suspect receives a copy of the Book of Evidence, and pleads guilty or not guilty to the charges. If the suspect does not have legal representation at this stage, the Court may appoint a solicitor to represent him.

The Book of Evidence must include the following:
- Details of the charge / charges against the accused
- Copies of witness statements
- List of witnesses the prosecution are going to call
- Statement of the evidence each of these witnesses is going to give
- List of exhibits

The District Court Judge hears the charges against the accused, and decides if the case is ready to go to trial. The accused enters a plea of guilty or not guilty to the charges. If the case is to be heard by the District Court, a trial date will be set. If the case is to be prosecuted in the Circuit Court or in the Central Criminal Court, the case will be forwarded to the relevant Court. Offences such as rape, rape under Section 4 or aggravated sexual assault must always be tried on indictment as provided for under Section 13 of the Criminal Procedure Act, 1967 (as amended by Section 20 of the Criminal

Law Rape Amendment Act, 1990).

The victim is not required to attend the District Court at this stage. It is important for the victim to be aware that her role in the case is that of a witness only. If the case is heard at the District Court and the accused pleads "not guilty", the victim is required to give evidence under oath.

If a case is forwarded to the Circuit Court or Central Criminal Court, a date will be set by that Court to hear the case. This date is determined by the waiting list of cases, in the relevant Court. The case is rarely heard on this date and there are usually a number of adjournments before a final date is set to hear the case. It may take up to 2 years from the date the offence is reported to the Gardaí to the date the trial commences at the Circuit Court or Central Criminal Court. The Office of the DPP will appoint a legal team to prosecute the case. The defendant's solicitor will engage barristers to defend the case.

5. The Plea

The accused may have admitted his guilt or declared his innocence to the Gardaí during questioning. At the District Court he may plead guilty or not guilty to the charges. The accused may change his plea to the Court. If the accused pleads guilty a trial is not necessary and the accused will be referred to the appropriate Court for sentencing.

In some cases the solicitor for the accused /defendant may approach the prosecution offering to plead guilty to fewer charges or to a lesser charge. This is commonly known as *Plea-Bargaining*, a term which is not officially provided for or recognised in Irish Law. The Office of the DPP has laid down clear guidelines for pre-trial discussions concerning pleas.

The DPP is not obliged to consult the victim during these negotiations.

6. The Trial

It can take an average of two years from the time of reporting the assault to the Gardaí and the case coming to court. When the trial date is set the Gardaí informs the victim of the date and issues a summons to the victim to attend court to give evidence. Although the assault happened to the victim, his or her status in court is that of a witness to the crime. The victim is not entitled to legal representation except in special circumstances, namely when the defence requests permission to question the victim on her past sexual history. In this event, the victim is entitled to free legal aid to contest the request. The jury are requested to leave the courtroom when this issue is being argued and decided upon. When this issue has been decided upon the jury return to the courtroom and the Legal Aid solicitor is discharged.

At the start of a trial a **jury** is sworn in. Every citizen between the age of 18 and 70 years can be called for jury service. Exceptions are those working within the court service, the Gardaí, the armed forces, anyone suffering from a disability that would make it difficult for them to participate, and those with a criminal conviction. A jury is made up of 12 people. The prosecution and each accused person can challenge up to seven jurors without having to give a reason. If challenged, the juror is excluded from serving on the jury. In addition, other jurors can be challenged by the prosecution and the accused, but the jurors can then only be excluded if compelling reasons can be given. When the jury is finally chosen they must choose a foreman/woman before the start of the trial. This person will deliver the verdict when the trial is concluded. The DPP will have engaged a barrister to argue the case on behalf of the Office of the DPP. The victim, as a witness in the case will not have been involved in preparing the case for prosecution. The victim may meet the legal team conducting the prosecution on the date the trial starts. This meeting is arranged by the Gardaí. The victim will not have had any contact with the Office of the DPP, prior to the date of the trial. This meeting is usually very brief as the legal team will be mindful of an accusation of being seen to influence or counsel a witness.

Though most criminal prosecutions are heard in public, in serious sexual offence cases, such as rape or aggravated sexual assault, the trial judge can, because of the circumstances of the case, exclude everyone from the court, except officers of the court, persons directly concerned in the proceedings (which would obviously include the complainant), and representatives of the press. The verdict and sentence will still however be pronounced in public. Furthermore sexual offence complainants have a right to anonymity in respect of criminal proceedings, though a trial judge may lift this restriction if it would induce potential witnesses to come forward, and the accused's case would be adversely affected if the restriction was not lifted. The trial judge may also vary the restriction if he or she believes it is imposing a substantial and unreasonable restriction on the reporting of the proceedings. It should also be noted that there is also a restriction on publishing matters likely to lead to the identification of an accused, charged with rape. This restriction ends, among other things, if the accused waives the right, or if he is found guilty of the offence.

When the trial starts the victim is usually the first to be called to give evidence. The victim is first questioned by the barrister engaged by the DPP to prosecute the case and then questioned by the barrister for the accused. This is called **cross-examination**. Recalling and recounting the assault in a courtroom in the presence of the accused is a traumatic experience for a victim. The Irish legal system is an adversarial system. The role of the defence barrister is to attempt to discredit evidence given by the victim. When the victim has finished giving evidence the barrister engaged by the Office of the DPP, calls other witnesses, including the first person the victim told of the assault, (which will be particularly relevant if the prosecution wishes to rely on the **doctrine of recent complainant**, that is that the complainant is a credible and consistent witness) the Garda, the doctor who conducted the FME, and other witnesses who can corroborate the victims version of the assault. These witnesses are cross-examined by the defence. The defence may call additional witnesses, for example they might call an expert witness to challenge medical evidence. The accused person does not have to give evidence and no adverse inference can be drawn by the judge or jury by this refusal or failure. Nor will the jury normally be aware of any previous convictions which the accused might have.

When all the evidence has been heard, each barrister will make a closing statement. The judge will sum up the facts of the case for the jury and instruct them on the law. The jury will then leave the court and retire to the jury room to consider the evidence before them and decide if the accused is guilty or not guilty of the charges. A trial of rape or sexual assault typically lasts 5 to 6 days.

7. Verdict

If the jury finds the accused/defendant not guilty, then he is free to go. A verdict of not guilty means that the jury was not able to establish **beyond reasonable doubt** that the perpetrator committed the offence he was charged with. Frequently this decision centres on the issue of consensual sexual activity.

8. Sentencing

When an accused person is found guilty of a crime either by a jury or by pleading guilty, a date is set for sentencing. The judge must decide on a punishment by taking into consideration the individual circumstances of each case. In order to assist in the sentencing decision the judge may request a *victim impact report*. A victim impact report is compiled by a counsellor, psychologist, doctor, Garda, or by the victim herself, and outlines how the assault has impacted on the victims life and how it may do so in the future. The victim may also speak directly to the judge on the impact / effects of the assault. The report/statement cannot be used to engage in a re-trial of the case, or introduce evidence not admitted at trial, or to select the punishment the victim thinks appropriate for the crime.

The judge may request a probation or psychiatric report on the offender before passing sentence and considers what is termed **mitigating factors**, such as age, state of health, previous offences, whether he pleaded guilty at an early stage, likelihood of re-offending etc. The accused is also permitted to have evidence of his good character, if applicable, admitted as a mitigating factor at sentencing stage. The judge will be informed of any previous convictions the offender may have.

The judge will hand down a prison sentence or a non-custodial sanction having regard to the statutory maxima applicable and the circumstances of the individual case. If, for example, an offender is placed on probation, the offender may be subject to a number of terms and may receive a prison sentence if he breaches the terms of his probation. A suspended sentence is also subject to terms set out by the judge. The length of sentences vary, depending on the charges and on the individual circumstances of the case and of the offender. If the victim or the Office of the DPP is of the opinion that the sentence is too lenient, the victim,a family member, the victims doctor or solicitor may write to the DPP to ask him to **appeal the leniency of the sentence**. The convicted offender can also appeal against the verdict or the severity of the sentence, depending on the offence. The judge will order the convicted offender to be placed on the Register of Sex Offenders, for a specified period.

9. Sex Offender Register (Sex Offenders Act 2001)

While the term **Sex Offenders Register** is commonly used in Ireland there is in fact no such register. Upon conviction for a sexual offence to which the register applies, the court is required to issue a certificate which states that the convicted person is now subject to the requirements of the Sex Offenders Act, 2001. Copies of this certificate are then sent to the Gardaí, the convicted offender, and the Governor of the prison to which the offender is sent (if a custodial sanction is imposed). The Garda Domestic Violence and Sexual Assault Unit also receive a copy of the Sex Offenders Notification Form from the Garda station in whose area the sex offender resides. This certificate states that the convicted person is now subject to the requirements of the Sex Offenders Act, 2001. The Garda Domestic Violence and Sexual Assault Unit also receive a copy of the **Sex Offenders Notification Form** from the Garda station in whose area the sex offender resides.

The Garda Domestic Violence and Sexual Assault Unit in Dublin keep a record of every registered sex offender, convicted in Ireland. Each local Garda Station maintains information on registered sex offenders in their area. A registered sex offender, on release from prison, is required to report to the local Gardaí and register his address. He is also obliged to notify the Gardaí if he is changing address or leaving the country for any reason including vacations. Victims are not automatically informed about the release date of an offender. If a victim or their family write to the relevant prison authority they will be advised of the expected release date.

As a result of the Sex Offenders Act, 2001, those who are convicted of certain sexual offences are now obliged to provide certain information to the Gardaí including the address at which they are living following their release from prison. The list of sexual offences which are subject to the Act include Rape; Sexual Assault; Aggravated Sexual Assault; Incest; Sexual offences against mentally impaired persons; Defilement of a girl under 15 years; Defilement of a girl 15 – 17 years; Offences under the Child Trafficking and Pornography Act, 1998; and sexual offences committed outside Ireland contrary to Sexual Offences (Jurisdiction) Act, 1996.

In the case of sexual assault and incest, the Sex Offenders Act 2001 does not apply if the victim or other party to the offence was aged 17 years or more when the offence was committed and the person convicted has not been sentenced to any punishment involving imprisonment or made subject to any measures involving deprivation of liberty.

In the case of defilement of a child aged under 17 years, the Act does not apply if the offender is not more than two years older than the victim. This provision is set out in Section 3 of the Criminal Law (Sexual Offences) Act, 2006.

10. Appeal

Should a defendant disagree with the verdict or sentence of a criminal court, then the possibility of an appeal may be available. Defendants found guilty in the District Court may appeal to the Circuit Court against conviction and severity of punishment or against severity alone. Those found guilty and sentenced in the Circuit Court or the Central Criminal Court may appeal to the Court of Criminal Appeal, against conviction and severity of punishment, severity only, and conviction only.

If acquitted, the accused cannot be tried again for the same offence. If, however, the accused has been convicted and sentenced but there is a perception that the sentence imposed was unduly lenient, it is possible for the Director of Public Prosecutions to appeal the undue leniency of the sentence provided the case was tried on indictment. In cases where an accused has been acquitted, it may also be possible for the Director of Public Prosecutions or the Attorney General to refer a question of law to the Supreme Court having consulted with the trial judge. This referral, however, will not affect the verdict in favour of the accused.

4. Frequently Asked Questions

Chapter 4
Frequently Asked Questions

Reporting to the Gardaí

Is there a time limit on reporting a rape to the Gardaí?

There is no time limit on reporting to the Gardaí. However, the chances of building a strong case against your assailant are improved if you report sooner rather than later. Early reporting allows for the collection of any physical evidence and it also can be used at the trial to show consistency on your part.

What should I do if I think I have been drugged?

Call into your local Garda Station as soon as possible. If the assault took place less than 72 hours before, the Garda in charge of your case will ask for a urine sample to test for any drugs that you have ingested against your will (e.g. spiked drinks). The Garda will stand outside the bathroom door while you give your sample and then send your sample off to be tested.

Formal Statement of Complaint

If I am under 18 do my parents have to be present when giving my statement?

It is desirable for one of your parents or legal guardians to be present when giving a statement but it is not a legal requirement. In circumstances where the perpetrator is a parent or guardian, he will not be present when you give your statement.

Why are the Gardaí asking me so many questions about my past?

The Gardaí will try to gather as much information as possible before sending your case to the DPP. This may include questions about your sexual history which may seem intrusive and irrelevant. The DPP will want to know about anything that the defence team will also know and could affect the case. If, for example, the accused discloses information about you that the Gardaí are unaware of, it may be used to discredit you and your evidence, in court.

Do I have to answer these questions about my sexual history?

The Gardaí will advise you that it is best to answer all their questions fully and truthfully and to disclose any information that could be relevant to the case. As noted above, your answers to these questions may help obtain a successful prosecution.

Can I take a break during the interview?

You can take a break at any time while giving your statement.

Am I entitled to a copy of my statement?

You are entitled to a copy of your own statement at any time. If you are not given a copy, you should request one from the Gardaí. If the case does come to trial, you will be questioned on the information in your statement so it is important to be familiar with it. By the time a case comes to court, you may have forgotten some of the details in your statement which could raise doubts about your reliability as a witness.

The Investigation

When is the accused interviewed by the Gardaí?

The Gardaí will gather as much evidence as possible (interviewing witnesses, viewing CCTV data etc.) before interviewing the accused. This can take days, weeks or months depending on several factors including the Gardaí's workload, the number of witnesses to be interviewed, waiting on forensic results etc.

How long can the accused be questioned by the Gardaí?

The Gardaí can normally detain the accused for a maximum of 24 hours without charge.

Can the accused refuse to say anything or be examined for forensic evidence?

In general, no adverse inference can be drawn from a refusal by an accused to say anything to the Gardaí. A refusal in some instances, however, may permit a court to draw such inferences as appear proper. Such an adverse inference will have corroborative value. In other words it will act as independent evidence to support the prosecution case against the accused. For example, if an accused fails to mention certain facts to the Gardaí during questioning or on being charged, which he later relies upon in his defence at trial, the court can draw an adverse inference from this failure by the accused.

As regards forensic evidence, a failure by an accused to give consent for certain intimate bodily samples (such as blood, urine, pubic hair, or a swab from a bodily orifice or genital region) to be taken may result in the Court drawing an adverse inference. This again may amount to corroboration of any evidence to which the refusal is material. The Gardaí do not require the consent of an accused to take a non-intimate sample such as saliva, a hair, a nail, any material found under a nail, a swab from any part of the body other than a body orifice or a genital region.

Who will the Gardaí talk to during the investigation?

The Gardaí will interview the victim, the accused and any witnesses who may have information about the assault.

If I have to identify my assailant, do I really have to touch his shoulder?

No. A formal identification parade will be formed in a Garda station and each person will have a number. You will have to state the number in front of the person you believe assaulted you or point to him. However, there are no two-way mirrors in Gardaí stations so you will have to be in the same room as the accused in order to identify him.

What if the accused refuses to partake in a formal identification parade?

If the accused refuses to partake in a formal identification parade, the Gardaí may arrange an informal identification. This may involve pointing him out on the street.

Will the accused be required to participate in a formal identification parade if he is well known to me?

A formal parade is not required if the accused is well known to you.

Forensic Medical Examination (SATU)

What is the Sexual Assault Treatment Unit (SATU)?

SATU is a specialised unit in the hospital that performs forensic examinations on people who have been recently sexually assaulted.

Where is the Cork SATU?

SATU is located in the South Infirmary Victoria Hospital, Old Blackrock Road, Cork.

What are the access hours of SATU?

Doctors are on call for SATU 365 days a year 24 hours a day.

I had a shower a few hours ago, is there any point in having a forensic medical examination?

Yes. Although it is preferable to have the examination before showering, the doctor may still be able to collect evidence for up to 7 days after the assault.

How long will I have to wait to be examined in SATU?

SATU doctors are on call 24 hours a day to perform forensic examinations. However, you will have to wait until the doctor on call arrives in SATU. Sometimes this can take less than two hours but other times you might have to wait up to six or eight hours to be examined.

Can I request a female doctor?

If a male doctor is on call and you wish to have a female doctor, you will have to wait until a female doctor can be arranged. This may take up to one day.

Will I have to pay for the examination?

No. The examination, emergency contraception and STI (Sexually transmitted infections) testing are free.

Do I have to be referred to SATU by the Gardaí?

No. You may be referred by your GP, the Sexual Violence Centre Cork, a Rape Crisis Centre, an A&E department or you may self refer. However, the Gardaí must be present for the forensic examination and the collection of any samples.

What if I don't want to report to the Gardaí but want to be examined for injuries, STIs and emergency contraception, can I go to SATU?

You may still attend SATU to receive a medical examination, emergency contraception and STI screening but any forensic examination will require the presence of the Gardaí.

Can I refuse to have the forensic examination?

Yes, however, the Gardaí will encourage you to have the examination so that all possible forensic evidence can be collected.

Are children examined at SATU?

Children under 14 years of age are not examined in SATU. The Health Service Executive (HSE) operate the service in respect of children under 14.

Do I have to sign a consent form?

Yes. All clients must sign a consent form before the forensic examination can begin.

If I am under 18 do my parents have to sign a consent form?

Yes. Both you and your parents or legal guardian must sign a consent form before the examination.

If I have other injuries will the doctors treat me in SATU or will I have to go to the A & E?

If you are seriously injured the doctors will refer you to A & E before they will perform the forensic examination.

Who is present during the forensic examination of the victim?

The doctor and nurse conducting the examination and a Garda will always be present during the examination. The Garda remains behind a screen to receive forensic samples from the doctor. A friend, family member or support worker may wait for you in a nearby waiting room at your request.

How long will the examination take?

The examination can last up to two hours.

Will the doctor take photographs?

Photographs are not taken routinely but may be taken if there are bite marks, cigarette burns etc. The Gardaí may take photographs of injuries to the face, head limbs etc. Photographs will not be taken without your permission.

Can I tell the doctor to stop if I am feeling too uncomfortable?

If at any time you do not wish to continue with the examination or if you are uncomfortable about a certain part of the examination, you may ask the doctor to stop, or you may take a break.

What happens to the evidence collected during the examination?

After the doctor has performed the medical examination and collected any evidence, a Garda seals and labels the samples and forwards them to the Forensic Science Laboratory in Dublin for analysis.

Will I get the results of the forensic tests?

No. The Gardaí will receive the results of your examination.

Will the Gardaí take the clothes I was wearing during the assault?

Yes. The Gardaí will send your clothes to the Forensic Science Laboratory in Dublin be tested for any evidence. You will be given a temporary change of clothes when the examination is finished. If you have already changed your clothes before you report to the Gardaí, put them in a paper bag and bring them with you.

Will I get my clothes back?

If the Gardaí have taken your clothes for forensic examination you can request the return of your clothes after the trial is over or if the DPP decides not to prosecute. Depending on the kinds of tests the forensic laboratory has performed on your clothes they may not be in the same state as when you gave them to the Gardaí.

Can I get prescriptions for sleeping pills/anti-depressants in SATU?

SATU will not prescribe sleeping pills or anti-depressants. These can be prescribed by your GP.

Can I get the morning after pill?

Yes. The doctor will supply medication to prevent pregnancy, free of charge.

Can I get tested for sexually transmitted infections (STI)?

Yes. The doctor will test for STIs and will give you a follow up appointment at SATU when results are available.

Can I have a shower in SATU after the examination?

Yes. You can shower after the examination and the hospital will give you a change of clothes.

Is counselling/support provided?

The Sexual Violence Centre Cork and Rape Crisis Centres offer crisis support to anyone attending SATU. The Centres also offer short and long term counselling and support after the SATU examination.

File Goes to the DPP

How long does it take before the Investigation file is sent to the DPP?

The gathering of evidence can take months or longer. If you are reporting past abuse, gathering evidence may be more complex. It will take time to retrieve old medical reports and/or to interview people who may be relevant in the case. The Garda dealing with your case will also have other duties to perform and this can result in a delay in completing the Investigation File.

Who can I talk to about the status of my case?

The investigating Gardaí should keep you informed on the progress of the investigation and the progress of the prosecution.

Decision on Prosecution

How long does it take for the DPP to make a decision regarding prosecution?

The DPP may make a decision within two weeks of receiving the Investigation File from the Gardaí. However, a decision may take longer if the case is complex, if there is a large volume of material to be considered, if there is more than one accused or if more information is requested by the DPP.

Can the DPP decide not to prosecute if there has been a long delay in reporting?

The DPP has discretion not to proceed with a prosecution and the courts may refuse to allow a trial to proceed in cases where there has been a long delay in reporting. This is because it is deemed that a long delay can make it unreasonably unfair for the accused to defend himself. If a trial does go ahead after a long delay, the judge will give a warning to the jury about the difficulties facing the accused in defending himself after a long period of time. In some instances, the delay in proceeding with a prosecution is as a result of a relationship of authority or dominion. This is most likely to arise in the context of Sexual Offences committed by an adult against a child. The risk of an unfair trial in such circumstances is not the fault of the person complaining, but of the person who created the relationship of authority or dominion (including parents, guardians, older siblings or other adults in a close relationship with the child). Each case is considered on its individual merits.

Can I find out the reasons why the DPP decides not to prosecute a case?

No. The DPP does not give reasons to victims for this decision not to prosecute a case. This policy is presently under review by the Office of the DPP. The Gardaí will be informed of the reasons but are not permitted to disclose this information.

Can the DPP's decision not to prosecute be changed?

The victim, victim's family, doctor, lawyer or social worker can write to the DPP to request that the file be reviewed. A review will only be conducted where new evidence has come to light.

Pre Trial

What if the accused doesn't turn up for court?

The judge may issue a warrant for his arrest.

Will my name be revealed at the District Court hearing?

You have the right not to be identified in public hearings or in the media at any time. The charges against the accused will be read out as a number and your name will not be mentioned.

What is the Book of Evidence?

The Book of Evidence includes: a statement of the charges made against the accused; a copy of any sworn information in writing; a list of the witnesses the prosecution is going to call; evidence the prosecution thinks witnesses will give in court; the list of exhibits that are to be introduced at trial (any physical evidence such as photographs or weapons, that will be used in court; any forensic evidence collected; other documents to be used in court), and the statement of the accused (if one was made).

Who receives a copy of the Book of Evidence?

The Gardaí, the District Court Judge and the accused receive a copy of the Book of Evidence. The victim is not entitled to see the Book of Evidence.

How long does it take to prepare a Book of Evidence?

The amount of time required for the preparation of a Book of Evidence can vary greatly depending on the complexity of the case. It should however be completed within 42 days of the accused being charged with the offences. Extensions of time can however be granted for the Book of Evidence to be prepared.

Can additions be made to the Book of Evidence after it has been given to the accused and the judge?

Yes. The Office of the DPP can serve the accused with any additional documents (such as a list of any further witnesses) that are then added to the Book of Evidence. There is no time limit as to when these documents can be served on the accused but the trial may be postponed if they are served too close to the start of the trial.

Is the accused usually allowed out of jail while he is waiting for the case to go to trial?

Yes. Once a person has been arrested and charged, he is entitled to be released on bail unless the prosecution can argue that there are special circumstances that should prevent a bail application. These special circumstances would include the possibility that the accused would commit a further serious offence whilst on bail, run away and not return for the trial, and/or try to interfere with witnesses or destroy or conceal evidence.

How long should it take for my case to go to trial?

If the accused pleads not guilty, it will usually take about two years for your case to come to trial. However, if the accused is in custody the trial could start sooner.

Can I meet with the Prosecuting Barrister or State Solicitor in the months before the trial?

You may request a pre-trial meeting with the Prosecuting Barrister or State Solicitor. They should explain what will happen in court but cannot discuss the evidence you will give in court. Often times, the victim will meet the State Solicitor and Prosecuting Barrister for the first time on the day of the trial.

What can I do if I or my family are contacted by the accused or his family?

Report the incident immediately to the Gardaí. This may be viewed as intimidating a witness and is a crime punishable up to a maximum of ten years in prison.

What is a Plea Bargain?

Plea-bargaining is the term given to the negotiation that occurs between the State and the accused. In this negotiation the accused seeks to secure a lesser sentence in return for a guilty plea. In practice, the defendant's solicitor may ask the prosecution to consider changing a more serious charge to a lesser charge on the condition that he pleads guilty. The Defence may also indicate that they will plead guilty to a number of the offences with which they are charged. For example, an accused is charged with ten offences and he is willing to plead to five if the State drops the other five charges. The prosecutor will inform the DPP and take direction from the office of the DPP.

Is the victim asked or informed when a plea bargain is considered by the DPP?

The DPP is not obliged to consult the victim before agreeing to a plea bargain.

Can the judge dismiss a case if too much time has passed? Does this happen in practice?

Delay in a case can be unfair to the accused, making it difficult for him to prepare a defence. Delay therefore can constitute a basis for preventing a prosecution case from proceeding. This will usually be by way of judicial review where the accused will seek an order prohibiting the prosecution from proceeding with the case. Excessive delay can be brought about either through the State failing to progress the prosecution case or from a failure on the part of the victim to lodge a complaint within a reasonable time. For indictable Offences, there is no statutory period of limitation as to when a case will be time-barred. The delay must however be excessive and it must be shown to prejudice the accused's right to a fair trial.

The Trial

Why are some cases heard in different courts?

Generally speaking, the more serious the crime, the higher the court at which the trial is heard. The District Court is the lowest court in Ireland. Sexual assaults of a less serious nature are tried here by a judge only. Sexual assault cases are tried in the Circuit Criminal Court. Rape, Rape Under Section 4 and aggravated sexual assault are tried in the Central Criminal Court.

How many days on average does a trial take?

The average length of a rape trial is six days. The trial can take longer depending on the number of witnesses and other evidence.

Who is allowed in the courtroom during the trial?

Most trials are open to the public; however, rape trials are heard in camera. This means that the general public is usually not allowed to be in the courtroom. The judge hearing the case almost always excludes from the Court everyone except the officers of the court, people directly concerned with the case (witnesses, barristers etc.) and representatives of the press. The victim and the accused may also have a parent, friend, relative or support worker accompany them to provide support.

When are witnesses allowed in the court room?

Generally, witnesses are permitted to be present in the court room for the entire trial. An application could be made to the trial judge to exclude a witness from the court, if it was felt that the witness would change his or her evidence as a result of what he or she would have already heard in court.

Will details of the case be published in the media?

Members of the press will be at the trial and can report on the trial. However, they are not allowed to publish any information that might reveal your identity or the identity of the accused charged with rape. If the accused is convicted, his name and the sentence will published by the media but your name will not. If he is related to you, his name will not be published except upon your request.

Will I have to see him in the courtroom?

Yes. He will be in the courtroom throughout the trial. Under special circumstances the judge may allow you to give your evidence in another room by way of a video link.

What is a video link?

If you are under 18 years of age, have a learning disability or if you feel you may be traumatised by giving evidence in the same room as your attacker, it is possible to give evidence in separate room from the court-room. The lawyers can ask you questions and the evidence is transmitted to the courtroom via live television link. A court official is present in the video room during this time.

Can my past sexual history be brought up in court?

Information on your past sexual history can only be brought up in court if the judge believes that it would be unfair to the accused to refuse to allow the evidence. The defence lawyer must make a special application to introduce the evidence to the judge without the presence of the jury. You are entitled to separate legal representation for such applications.

Why can't I have my own solicitor?

In Ireland, the victim of a sexual crime does not have a right to separate legal representation. The DPP prosecutes the person who assaulted you on behalf of the State and not on your behalf. You will be called by the DPP to give evidence as a *witness* for the State.

You make seek advice or information from a solicitor. However, it is important to note that he/she cannot act for you in any official way during the investigation or trial, except if an application is made by the defence to bring up your sexual history. In these circumstances, you are entitled to free legal aid for that specific application.

Why does the accused have a legal team?

The accused's rights to legal representation in a criminal trial is safeguarded under the Irish Constitution and the European Convention on Human Rights.

What if the only evidence against the accused is my testimony?

Cases will sometimes go ahead for prosecution with no other evidence than a victim's testimony. However, the judge can give a warning to the jury about the dangers of convicting a person based solely on victim testimony. The judge will decide whether to give a warning to the jury after considering the content and quality of the evidence and the circumstances of the case.

Can the accused refuse to give evidence in court?

Yes. The accused can refuse to testify in court and the jury is not allowed to make any judgements about this.

Will the jury be informed if the accused has previous convictions?

The jury will not usually be informed of the accused's previous convictions.

Sentencing

How much time passes between the trial and the sentencing?

Usually between one and three months will pass before a convicted offender is sentenced. This gives the trial judge time to review psychiatric or probation reports and the Victim Impact Report.

What factors will be taken into account in sentencing?

A judge must impose a sentence, which is appropriate for the particular crime *and* is appropriate for the particular circumstances of the individual being sentenced. A mix of aggravating and mitigating circumstances can be taken into account by the sentencing judge. Circumstances aggravating the offences could, among other things, include: premeditation, use of a weapon, the exploitation of a weak or defenceless victim, the use of excessive cruelty, and committing the offences for pleasure or excitement. Mitigating personal circumstances of an offender could include: his or her age, circumstances relating to family and life opportunities, the lack of a previous criminal record, whether a guilty plea has been entered, whether he or she has shown genuine remorse, and the consequences of the offences on the offender.

What is a *Victim Impact Report*?

When a defendant is found guilty of a sexual offence, the judge will request a Victim Impact Report to help decide on a sentence. The report outlines the ways in which the assault has affected the victim's life.

Who can write a *Victim Impact Report*?

A doctor, Garda, psychologist or counsellor may write this report on your behalf or you may choose to write one yourself. If you write it yourself it is referred to as a Victim Impact Statement.

Can the DPP appeal a sentence?

Yes. The DPP can appeal a sentence to the Court of Criminal Appeal within 56 days if he believes the trial judge to have been unduly lenient in light of all the circumstances.

Who can request the DPP to appeal a sentence?

The victim or a family member of the victim can write to the DPP to request him/her to appeal a sentence. Lawyers, doctors or social workers can also write to the DPP on behalf of their clients regarding an appeal of a sentence.

Will he be in custody between the time he is found guilty and the date of sentencing?

Sometimes he will be kept in custody until sentencing but other times he will be free until sentencing. The decision to keep him in jail until sentencing is dependant upon the circumstances of each individual case. The accused may also seek leave to appeal a guilty verdict.

Can the accused appeal a sentence and how does that happen?

If the accused is found guilty and believes that the sentence was unduly harsh, his solicitor can apply for a leave to appeal from the judge. The accused may also seek leave to appeal a guilty verdict.

Am I entitled to compensation?

The judge may order the defendant to compensate you for injuries or loss of income depending upon his income. The amount awarded to you cannot be more than you would be entitled to in a civil case. You may also claim compensation from the Criminal Injuries Compensation Tribunal.

What is the Criminal Injuries Compensation Tribunal?

It is a scheme funded by the Department of Justice Equality and Law Reform to compensate victims of violent crimes for expenses and losses suffered as a result of violent crime. You must apply to the Tribunal within three months of the date of the crime. If you were living in the same house as the person who committed the crime against you, you are not entitled to any compensation from the Tribunal.

After the Trial

If the offender is in prison, will I be notified when he is released?

According to the Victims Charter, Gardaí are supposed to notify you when the offender is due to be released from prison. This will also depend on the Prison Service notifying the Gardaí of an early release or temporary release.

Is the offender allowed to come near me after he has been released?

There is no legal way to prevent him from contacting you after he has been released. If he tries to harass you, intimidate you or assault you, contact the Gardaí immediately.

What factors are taken into account when an offender who has been convicted is offered temporary release?

The Criminal Justice Act 1960 provides for the temporary release of persons from prison. This may be for one day release, overnight periods or for a lengthy period. Each person released is subject to the following conditions: to keep the peace and be of good behaviour during the release period; to be of sober habits; not to communicate or publish any matter by means of newspapers or any other publishing medium or to engage in public controversy.

Under the Prison Act, 2007, provision is now made for the Minister for Justice, Equality and Law Reform to make an order releasing a prisoner from custody for a specified period and purpose. This release will usually be granted on compassionate grounds, for the purpose of assessing prisoner's suitability for early release or his reintegration into society, or to enable a prisoner to assist in an investigation.

Will the offender have to serve his full sentence?

Provision for remission is contained under Rule 38 of the Rules for the Government of Prisons 1947 which provide that "a convicted person sentenced to imprisonment... shall be eligible, by industry and good conduct, to earn a remission of a portion of his imprisonment, not exceeding one fourth of the whole sentence".

Civil Cases

How expensive is a civil case?

In order to commence proceedings for a civil claim, you must hire a solicitor. The solicitor must advise you in writing of the fees he/she will charge you for his/her services. Usually if you win your case, most or all of your costs (including legal fees) will be paid for by the other party. However, if you lose, it is likely you will be obliged to pay all the costs and fees of your own legal team *and* that of the other party.

The District Court can award up to €6,348.69 in damages. The Circuit Court has can award up to €38,092 in damages. The High Court has unlimited power to award damages.

If your case is heard in Circuit Court and you are awarded less than €6,349 in damages or in the High Court and you are awarded less than €38,092 in damages, you may be penalised in costs. This means that even though you have won your case, you may be obliged to pay the extra costs incurred by both sides by having the case heard in the higher court. In normal circumstances 2 years is the limit for an action for damages arising from personal injuries iccured as an adult. It is advisable to contact a solicitor for advice

Is a civil case in front of a judge only or is a jury present?

A civil case is heard only by a judge.

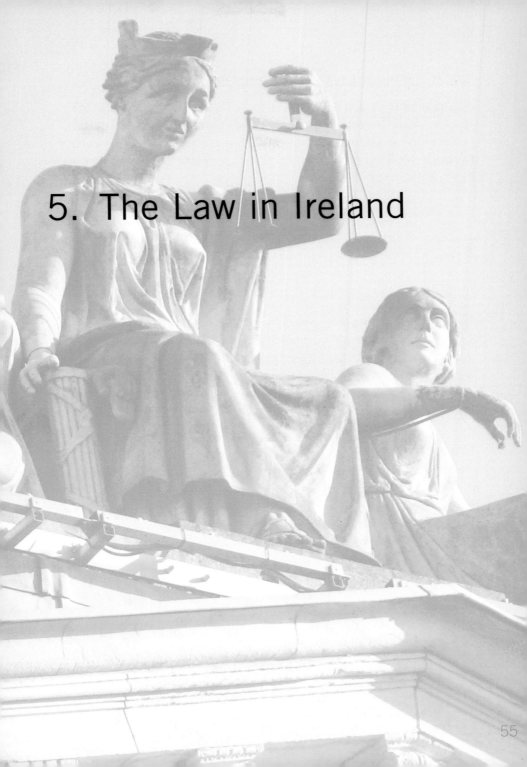

5. The Law in Ireland

Chapter 5
The Law in Ireland

The Offence of Rape

The current definition of rape is to be found in Section 2 (1) of the Criminal Law (Rape) Amendment Act 1981. It is stated here that the offence of rape is committed if a man has sexual intercourse with a woman who does not consent to it, and that he *knows* that she does not consent to the intercourse or is *reckless* as to this fact. Recklessness in this context means that the man must have been consciously aware of the possibility that the victim might not have been consenting. The fact that the woman was intoxicated (i.e., under the influence of alcohol or drugs) when the rape occurred does not automatically make her consent to sex invalid. However, if she was so intoxicated as to be incapable of giving a meaningful consent to sex, the court may hold that her apparent consent is invalid. Sexual intercourse for the purposes of rape means vaginal intercourse. There must be some penetration by the penis, however slight, and ejaculation is not necessary for proof of the offence. Rape is by definition only committed when a man has sexual intercourse with a woman without her consent. Therefore a woman cannot rape a man. However, under amended legislation, a man can rape a man.

Consent

Consent goes to the very heart of rape and is essentially the most important part of any complaint. For a successful rape conviction, the prosecution must prove beyond a reasonable doubt that the woman did not consent to the sexual intercourse. For a woman's consent to be valid, it must be real and clear, and not the result of any fraud or deception. A woman must be in a position to give consent, so if she is sleeping, or intoxicated (not merely drunk), this will not be the case. Contrary to what one might think, merely because a woman submits herself to the intercourse, and does not offer any struggle does not necessarily imply that she has consented. It has been well recognised in Ireland, by virtue of section 9 of The Criminal Law (Rape) Amendment Act 1990, that even if a woman did not physically resist, this does not constitute consent.

The Age of Consent

Since the enactment of the Criminal Law (Sexual Offences) Act 2006, the age of consent to penetrative sexual activity for both males and females now stands at seventeen. Males and females under seventeen are also legally incapable of consenting to any activity which would constitute an aggravated sexual assault. The legal age of consent to activity which would constitute a sexual assault is fifteen. The age of consent for this form of sexual activity is lower because the law on sexual assault was not affected by the 2006 Act.

Honest Belief Defence

It has been accepted by the law that a defendant might genuinely think that a woman is consenting, when in fact this is not the case. In these circumstances, the defendant ought to be acquitted. This has been confirmed by case law in England and by the legislature and case law in Ireland. The position is that where a man genuinely but mistakenly believes that a woman is consenting, he should not be guilty of the offence. The rationale for this is that the defendant does not have the requisite guilty mind for the commission of rape if he is genuinely but unreasonably mistaken as to the woman's consent. However, it must be remembered that at all times, despite such allegations of this position being a 'rapist's charter', a jury is not obliged to believe a defendant's claim of reasonable belief and may convict him if they do not believe the claim.

Section 4 Rape

The Criminal Law (Rape) (Amendment) Act, 1990 created a new offence known as 'rape under section 4'. It is an offence that can be committed by either a man or a woman. Rape under section 4 is a sexual assault that includes penetration of the anus or mouth by the penis, or the penetration of the vagina by an object held by another person. The Act also enables a jury to consider alternative verdicts in the event the evidence does not warrant a conviction for rape under section 4 but warrants a conviction for aggravated sexual assault or for sexual assault.

Sexual Activity with a Person under the Age of Consent

The Criminal Law (Sexual Offences) Act 2006 makes it an offence to engage in a 'sexual act' with a person who is under fifteen or seventeen. The reason for the different age categories is that the penalty on conviction is higher if the child against whom the offence is committed is under fifteen. The maximum penalty if found guilty of engaging in a sexual act with a child under 15 is life imprisonment; if the child is under 17, the maximum penalty is 5 years for the first offence and 10 years imprisonment for any subsequent offence. However, if the person convicted for a sexual act with a child under 17 is a person in authority (such as a parent, step-parent, guardian, or grandparent), then the maximum penalties available increase to 10 years imprisonment for the first offence and 15 years imprisonment for any subsequent offence. The term 'sexual act' refers to any sexual activity which would constitute rape, rape under section 4 or aggravated sexual assault. Since the children against whom these offences are committed are under the age of consent, consent or an honest belief in consent will not provide a defence. However, a person who is charged with an offence under the 2006 Act has a defence if s/he can prove that s/he honestly believed that the child with whom s/he engaged in the sexual act with had attained the age of fifteen or seventeen respectively.

Intercourse with Mentally Ill Persons

Intercourse with a person suffering with a mental illness has been made an offence under Section 5 of the Criminal Law (Sexual Offences) Act, 1993. This offence is not categorised as statutory rape but it is often appropriate to treat it as such, as the rationale for its introduction is essentially the same - for the protection of a certain group in society. The legislation created three Offences:

- Intercourse or attempted intercourse with a mentally impaired person.

- Buggery or attempted buggery with a mentally impaired person.

- Acts of gross indecency or attempted acts of same, with someone who is mentally impaired.

Mental impairment is defined by the legislation as a disorder of the mind which prevents a person from leading an independent life or leaves them particularly open to manipulation. There are two possible defences within the Act. The first is that no offence has been committed if the defendant is married to the mentally impaired person, or has reasonable grounds for suspecting that he/she might be married to that person. Secondly, if the person can show that he/she did not know that the person was suffering from a disorder of the mind, or had no reason to suspect so.

Sexual Assault

Section 2 of the Criminal Law (Rape) (Amendment) Act 1990 placed the offence formerly known as indecent assault on a statutory basis. There are two parts to this offence: there must be an intentional assault, and an aura of indecency. It has therefore been held that the prosecution must show that the accused:

- Intentionally assaulted the victim.

- That the assault, or the circumstances accompanying it, were capable of being viewed by right-minded people as being indecent.

- That the accused intended to commit such an assault as is referred to in the second point above.

There are two types of sexual assault: sexual assault where there is indecent contact, and where there is no indecent contact. It has been established that where there is no contact, an element of hostility must be present. Hostile here usually means some sort of compulsion. Where contact has actually occurred, there is no onus on the prosecution to prove any hostility or force. Assault in this context can mean merely moving towards someone in a suggestive manner, and may even ground a claim in a civil action if the DPP refuses to prosecute. Difficulties arise in defining what is and what is not 'indecent'. Some circumstances may be quite obviously indecent, e.g. trying to remove someone's clothing, whereas other situations may be harder to pinpoint. There have been certain criteria laid out however:

- Some circumstances are regarded as being inherently incapable of being regarded as indecent, e.g. removing someone's shoes, even if the accused confesses to having an obsession with shoes.

- Conversely, some situations will always be regarded as being truly indecent e.g. removing someone's clothes against her will, will always be inappropriate, regardless of the intention of the accused.

- In cases where the lines are blurred, the jury may have regard to any surrounding factors, in considering whether an assault is, in fact, indecent. This could include the relationship between the parties, e.g., for a parent to spank a child is not normally considered indecent.

- It is not a defence to show that the victim was unaware of the indecent nature of the assault, as assaults of this nature can be committed on sleeping and unconscious victims.

Aggravated Sexual Assault

Section 3 (1) of the Criminal Law Rape (Amendment) Act 1990 creates the offence of aggravated sexual assault. Basically this is Sexual Assault aggravated by serious violence, or the threat of serious violence, or is such as to cause injury, humiliation or degradation of a grave nature to the person assaulted.

Buggery

Section 2 of the Criminal Law (Sexual Offences) Act, 1993 legalised anal intercourse between consenting adults over seventeen. Non-consensual anal intercourse with an adult is now covered by rape under section 4. Anal intercourse with a person under the age of consent is now covered by the Criminal Law Sexual Offences Act, 2006.

Indecent Exposure

This offence has been criminalised pursuant to various Acts such as Section 4 of the Vagrancy Act 1824, the Summary Jurisdiction (Ireland) Act 1871, and Section 18 of the Criminal Law Amendment Act 1935. It has been defined as occurring whenever a man intentionally exposes his genitalia to a female in a public place, e.g., such as urinating and/or 'flashing'. There is no sexual motive required, or even any other sort of intention such as to insult or annoy. Central to this offence is that of the definition of a public place. The defendant must be capable of being seen by one other person for it to constitute a public place. So long as the incident occurs in a public place, the offence has been committed.

Outraging Public Decency

This is a common law offence, meaning that it is not expressly laid out in any legislation but has been developed over the years through case law. It is basically agreed that the offence has been committed whenever someone performs a lewd or disgusting act in public that is an outrage to public decency. What is lewd or disgusting is a matter for the jury to decide. It has been accepted that outrage must go beyond the boundaries of merely offending or even shocking reasonable people and everything will depend on the individual circumstances of each case. While the conduct must be deliberate, it is not necessary to prove an intention to outrage public decency.

Incest

The crime of incest is covered by legislation known as the Punishment of Incest Act 1908. The essence of this offence is sexual intercourse with a close blood relative. While abuse or violence may figure in a lot of cases of incest, this is not an essential element of the crime.

Section 1 of the Act deals with incest committed by a male, and makes it an offence for a man to have intercourse with a female, who he knows to be his granddaughter, daughter, sister or mother. Section 2 governs the situation in relation to females, and makes it a crime for a female over the age of seventeen to have sexual intercourse with a male, whom she knows to be her grandfather, father, uncle or son. The sections also cover half relationships, e.g. half sisters, or brothers. Intention and specific knowledge of the particular relationship is an essential feature of this offences. The Criminal Law (Incest Proceedings) Act 1995, makes this an arrestable offence, attracting a maximum penalty of life imprisonment when the incest has been carried out by a male and a maximum of seven years when it is carried out by a female. The offence does not apply to other familial relationships such as aunts, uncles, and nephews.

Consent is also no defence to incest. In the event of there being a consensual incestuous relationship between two adults, only one is charged; the other, however, may be charged as an accomplice. Furthermore, no offences is committed under section 2 by the female if the female is under 17 years of age, as women under that age are regarded as victims rather than offenders in this context.

Sexual Harassment

Sexual Harassment, under employment equality and equal status legislation, is defined as behaviour which is unwelcome and could be reasonably regarded as sexually offensive, humiliating or intimidating to the recipient. It can take the form of a physical, verbal or psychological attack and can be openly aggressive or subtly hidden.

Some examples of sexual harassment include:

- **Physical** - Unnecessary touching, pinching or brushing against another;
- **Verbal** - Unwelcome sexual advances, demands for sexual favours, suggestive remarks, innuendoes or lewd comments;
- **Non-Verbal** - Displays of pornographic or sexually suggestive pictures and objects; leering, whistling or sexually suggestive gestures.

Sexual harassment at work or school falls under the Employment Equality Act 1998, as amended and is dealt with by the Equality Tribunal.

Stalking

"Stalking" is not a legal term but can be described as a series of acts which are intended to cause harassment to another person and can be prosecuted under the Non Fatal Offences Against the Person Act 1997. Victims are subjected to constant harassment at home, in public places or work, to the extent that they feel they are no longer in control of their lives. Stalkers can pursue a victim by threatening, abusive or obscene phone calls; using abusive and threatening language; or committing acts of violence. Frequently, however, stalkers do not overtly threaten their victims, but use behaviour that appears routine and harmless. However, any behaviour which is persistently inflicted on a person against their will can be distressing and threatening.

If the case is brought to court, the judge may order that the stalker is not allowed to communicate with the victim in any way or that he must remain a certain distance away from the victim and breaking that order constitutes an offence. In addition to the judge's orders, a stalker may also face a fine and/or prison sentence.

Reckless Endangerment of Children

The Criminal Justice Act 2006 provides for a new offence of reckless endangerment of children. This offence may be committed by a person who has authority or control over a child or an abuser and who intentionally or recklessly endangers a child by:

- Causing or permitting any child to be placed or left in a situation which creates a substantial risk to the child of being a victim of serious harm or sexual abuse, or
- Failing to take reasonable steps to protect a child from such a risk while knowing that the child is in such a situation.

Child Trafficking and Pornography

The "http://www.irishstatutebook.ie/ZZA22Y1998.html" Child Trafficking and Pornography Act 1998 ,which is amended by"http://www.oireachtas.ie/documents/bills28/acts/2007/a607.pdf" Section 6 of the Criminal Law (Sexual Offences) (Amendment) Act 2007, deals with a number of offences involving children under the age of 17. These include:

- Child trafficking and taking a child for sexual exploitation
- Meeting a child for the purpose of sexual exploitation
- Allowing a child to be used for child pornography
- Producing, distributing, printing or publishing child pornography
- Possession of child pornography.

Arraignment

Irrespective of what level of court the case is heard in, it is when charges are read to the accused and he is asked if he is pleading guilty or not guilty.

Bail

The accused is allowed to go free on the condition that he will appear in court when required. The accused may have to pay money or arrange for someone else to guarantee his presence in court in order to be released on bail.

Barrister

Lawyer hired by the solicitor to prosecute or defend the case in court. Also known as 'Counsel'.

Book of Evidence

A file prepared by the State Solicitor that contains all the evidence collected by the Gardaí during the investigation.

Central Criminal Court

Hears cases of rape, rape under section 4, aggravated sexual assault and attempted aggravated assault by a judge and jury.

Circuit Court

Hears cases of sexual assault of a more serious nature than those in the District court.

Complainant

Legal term for the victim of sexual violence during a court case.

Consent

An active, conscious choice to participate in any sexual activity. Consent can be withdrawn at any time. A person cannot give their consent if she is asleep, substantially physically or mentally impaired due to alcohol or other drugs, unconscious, or if intimidated, forced, or threatened.

Date Rape Drugs

Can be used to assist a sexual assault. Also referred to as 'drug assisted rape' or 'drug facilitated sexual assault'. The drugs often have no colour, smell, or taste and are easily added to flavoured drinks without the victim's knowledge. Victims may be physically helpless, unable to refuse sex, and can't remember what happened. The most common are: GHB, Rohypnol (Roofies) and Ketamine (Special K).

Defendant/Accused

A person charged with a criminal offences

Disclosure

Telling someone about the assault.

District Court

The lowest court in Ireland which hears cases that are considered minor Offences by a judge only. The District Court is also the first court the defendant is brought to be formally charged.

DPP

Director of Public Prosecution decides whether to charge a person with a crime and what those charges should be. The DPP is in charge of the prosecution case throughout the legal process.

Emergency Contraception

Prescription drug that can prevent pregnancy if taken within 72 hours of unprotected sex. Also known as the morning after pill.

Forensic

Scientific technique used to examine evidence collected during an investigation.

In Camera

Means that the general public is excluded from the courtroom

Marital Rape

Any unwanted sexual acts by a spouse or ex-spouse, committed without consent and/or against a person's will, obtained by force, or threat of force, intimidation, or when a person is unable to consent.

Perpetrator

Person who commits the assault.

Plea

The response of 'guilty' or 'not guilty' by the accused when formally charged with a crime in court.

Plea Bargain

When the solicitor for the accused and the prosecution agree to a less serious charge in exchange for the accused pleading guilty.

Prosecution

Name for the entire team (Gardaí, Solicitors, Barristers and DPP) that is responsible for proving the guilt of the accused person. Also used to describe the process of proving someone committed a crime.

SATU

Sexual Assault Treatment Unit is a specialised unit, based in a hospital, where you can go if you have been sexually assaulted within the last seven days. The doctor and nurse will examine you and collect samples such as hair, semen, fibres or saliva that may be used as evidence in a Gardaí investigation and any future prosecution. Emergency contraception and STI screening are also available from SATU

Sexually Transmitted Infections (STI)

Infections that are spread through sexual activity. Also known as Sexually Transmitted Diseases (STDs)

Solicitor

Lawyer who gives legal advice to clients and prepares the case for the barrister.

State Solicitor

Represents the DPP in all court appearances as an aid to Counsel.

Statement

A detailed description by the victim in the presence of the Gardaí of the events that happened before, during and after the assault.

Victim Impact Report

Report prepared by victim, doctor, Garda, psychologist or counsellor that outlines the ways in which the assault has affected the victim's life.

Video Link

The witness gives evidence in a separate room from the regular courtroom and her testimony is transmitted to the courtroom via a live television link.

An Garda Síochána

Garda Headquarters
Phoenix Park, Dublin 8
Tel: 01 666 0000
Web: www.garda.ie
Includes listings of all Garda stations throughout
the country

Garda Domestic Violence and Sexual Assault Investigation Unit

Harcourt Square, Dublin 2
Contact is by referral only through the complainant's
local Garda station, where appropriate.

Garda Síochána Ombudsman Commission

150 Abbey Street Upper, Dublin 1
LoCall: 1890 600 800
Tel: 01 871 6727
Fax: 01 814 7023
E-mail: info@gsoc.ie
Web: www.gardaombudsman.ie

Office of the Director of Public Prosecutions

14-16 Merrion Street, Dublin 2
Tel: 01 678 9222
Fax: 01 661 0915
E-mail: dpp@dppireland.ie
Please note that for reasons of confidentiality the
Office of the Director of Public Prosecutions cannot
accept correspondence relating to criminal prosecution
files by e-mail. Any correspondence relating to criminal
prosecution files should be in writing and forwarded by
post to the above address.
Web: www.dppireland.ie

The Courts Service

15-24 Phoenix Street North
Smithfield, Dublin 7
Tel: 01 888 6000
Web: www.courts.ie

Department of Justice, Equality and Law Reform

94 St Stephen's Green, Dublin 2
LoCall: 1890 221 227
Tel: 01 602 8202
Fax: 01 661 5461
E-mail: info@justice.ie
Web: www.justice.ie

Law Society of Ireland

Blackhall Place, Dublin 7
Tel: 01 6724800
E-mail: general@lawsociety.ie

Legal Aid Board

Head Office, Quay Street
Cahirciveen, Co Kerry
Tel: 066 947 1000
Lo Call: 1890 615 200
E mail: info@legalaidboard.ie
DUBLIN OFFICE
47 Upper Mount Street, Dublin 2
Tel: 01 644 1900

Sexual Assault Treatment Units (SATUs)

Cork SATU

South Infirmary Victoria University
Hospital, Cork
Tel: 021 4926297
E-mail: satu@sivuh.ie

Dublin SATU

Rotunda Hospital, Parnell Street
Dublin 1
Tel: 01 873 0700 hospital administration
E-mail: satu@rotunda.ie

Letterkenny SATU
Letterkenny General Hospital
Letterkenny, Co Donegal
Tel: 074 25888 hospital administration
Fax: 074 22824

Waterford SATU
Waterford Regional Hospital
Dunmore Road, Waterford
Tel: 051 848000 hospital administration
Fax: 051 879495

Limited services are also available in Limerick and Tralee:

Limerick
Mid Western Regional Hospital
Dooradoyle, Limerick
Tel: 061 301111 all departments
         061 482120 accident and emergency
Fax: 061 301165

Tralee
Kerry General Hospital
Tralee, Co Kerry
Tel: 066 7184000 hospital administration
Fax: 066 7126241

New units will shortly be opening in Galway and Mullingar.

Rape Crisis Centres

Athlone Midlands Rape Crisis Centre
2 Fairview, Garden Vale, Athlone,
Co. Westmeath
Freephone: 1800 306 600
Business: 09064 73815
Fax: 09064 91888
E-mail: amrcc@eircom.net

Belfast Rape Crisis & Sexual Abuse Centre (N.I.)
29 Donegal St, Belfast BTI 2FG
Helpline: 04890 249696
Business: 04890 329002
Fax: 04890 329001
E-mail: eileencalder@hotmail.com

Carlow and South Leinster Rape Crisis and Counselling Centre
72 Tullow St, Carlow.
Freephone: 1800 727 737
Business: 05991 33344
Fax: 05991 33344
E-mail: southleinsterrapecc@eircom.net

CORK
Sexual Violence Centre Cork
5 Camden Place, Cork
Freephone: 1800 496 496
Business: 021 4505577
Fax: 021 4504690
E-mail: info@sexualviolence.ie
Web: www.sexualviolence.ie

Donegal Sexual Abuse and Sexual Violence Centre
13 St. Eunan's Close, Convent Rd,
Letterkenny, Co. Donegal
Freephone: 1800 448 844
Business: 074 912 8211
Fax: 074 912 0642
E-mail: rapecrisis@eircom.net

Dublin Rape Crisis Centre
70, Lower Leeson St, Dublin 2
Freephone: 1800 778 888
Business: 01 661 4911
Fax: 01 661 0873
E-mail: rcc@indigo.ie
Web: www.drcc.ie

Galway Rape Crisis Centre
7, Claddagh Quay, Galway
Helpline: 1850 355 355 / 091 589495
Business: 091 583149
Fax: 091 583148
E-mail: administrator@galwayrcc.org
Web: www.galwayrcc.org

Kerry Rape & Sexual Abuse Centre
5 Greenview Terrace, Princes Quay,
Tralee, Co. Kerry
Freephone: 1800 633 333
Business: 066 712 3122
Fax: 066 712 0247
E-mail: krcc@eircom.net
Web: www.krsac.com

Killkenny Rape Crisis and Counselling Centre

1, Golfview Terrace, Off Grangers Rd, Kilkenny
Freephone: 1800 478 478
Business: 056 775 1555
Fax: 056 775 1538
E-mail: kkrcc@eircom.net

Limerick Rape Crisis Centre

Rochville House, Punch's Cross, Limerick
Freephone: 1800 311 511
Business: 061 311511
Fax: 061 312682
E-mail: limerickrcc@oceanfree.net

Louth Rape Crisis and Sexual Abuse Centre

PO Box 72, 76 Clanbrassil St, Dundalk, Co. Louth
Freephone: 1800 212 122
Business: 042 933 9491
Fax: 042 938 1968
E-mail: rcsacne@eircom.net

Mayo Rape Crisis Centre

Newtown, Castlebar, Mayo
Freephone: 1800 234 900
Business: 094 902 5657
Fax: 094 902 7188
E-mail: mayorcc@eircom.net

Sligo Rape Crisis Centre

42 Castle St, Sligo
Freephone: 1800 750 780
Business: 07191 71188
Fax: 07191 71268
E-mail: info@srcc.ie

Tipperary Rape Crisis Centre

20 Mary St, Clonmel, Co. Tipperary
Freephone: 1800 340 340
Business: 052 27676
Fax: 052 29171
E-mail: trcc@eircom.net

Tullamore Sexual Abuse and Rape Crisis Counselling Service

4 Harbour View, Store Street, Tullamore, Co Offaly
Freephone: 1800 323 232
Business: 05793 22500
Fax: 05793 22501
E-mail: tullamorerapecrisiscentre @eircom.net

Waterford Rape & Sexual Abuse Centre

2A Waterside, Waterford
Freephone: 1800 296 296
Business: 051 873362
Fax: 051 850717
E-mail: wrcc@indigo.ie

Wexford Rape & Sexual Abuse Support Services

Clifford St, Wexford
Freephone: 1800 330 033
Business: 053 22722
Fax: 053 52853
E-mail: wexrapecrisis@eircom.net
Web: www.wexfordrapecrisis.com

Support Services

One in Four

2 Holles Street, Dublin 2
Tel: 01 662 4070
Fax: 01 611 4650
E-mail: oneinfour.org

National Crime Victims Helpline

Tel: 1850 211 407 / 01 479 0592
E-mail: crimevictimshelpline.ie
Web: crimevictimshelpline.ie
An Garda Síochána, Annual Report 2006, Dublin: An Garda Síochána (2007) (www.garda.ie)

Appendix 3

References

An Garda Síochána, Garda Charter for Victims of Crime, Dublin: An Garda Síochána (www.garda.ie)

Department of Health and Children, Rape/Sexual Assault: National Guidelines on Referral and Forensic Clinical Examination in Ireland, Dublin: Department of Health and Children (2005) (www.dohc.ie)

Department of Health and Children, Sexual Assault Treatment Services: A National Review, Dublin: Department of Health and Children (2005) (www.dohc.ie)

Garda Ombudsman, First Annual Report 2006, Dublin: Garda Síochána Ombudsman Commission (2007) (www.gardaombudsman.ie)

Garda Ombudsman, What you need to know, Dublin: Garda Síochána Ombudsman Commission (www.gardaombudsman.ie)

Leane M, Ryan S, Fennell C, Egan E, Attrition in Sexual Assault Offence Cases in Ireland: A Qualitative Analysis. Dublin: The Stationary Office (2001)

McGee H, Garavan R, de Barra M, Byrne J, Conroy, R, The SAVI Report, Sexual Abuse in Ireland: A National Study of Irish Experiences, Beliefs and Attitudes Concerning Sexual Violence, Dublin: Liffey Press (2002) (www.drcc.ie)

National Adult Literacy Agency, A Plain English Guide to Legal Terms, Dublin: National Adult Literacy Agency (2003) (www.nala.ie)

National Crime Council, An Examination of Time Intervals in the Investigation and Prosecution of Murder and Rape Cases in Ireland from 2002 to 2004, Dublin: The Stationary Office (2006) (www.crimecouncil.ie)

Office of the Director of Public Prosecutions, Annual Report 2006, Dublin: Office of the Director of Public Prosecutions (2007) (www.dppireland.ie)

Office of the Director of Public Prosecutions, Attending Court as a Witness, Dublin: Office of the Director of Public Prosecutions (2006) (www.dppireland.ie)

Office of the Director of Public Prosecutions, Guidelines for Prosecutors, Dublin: Office of the Director of Public Prosecutions (2006) (www.dppireland.ie)

Office of the Director of Public Prosecutions, The Role of the DPP, Dublin: Office of the Director of Public Prosecutions (2006) (www.dppireland.ie)

Rape Crisis Network Ireland, What Survivors Told Us, National Rape Crisis Statistics 2004, Dublin: Rape Crisis Network Ireland (2005) (www.rcni.ie)

The Courts Service, Annual Report 2006, Dublin: The Courts Service (2007) (www.courts.ie)